finding your rhythm

A Kids Guide to Becoming a Musician

sarah michaels

Copyright © 2023 by Sarah Michaels

All rights reserved.

No part of this book may be reproduced in any form or by any electronic or mechanical means, including information storage and retrieval systems, without written permission from the author, except for the use of brief quotations in a book review.

contents

Introduction	5
1. UNCOVERING YOUR MUSICAL INTEREST	13
Understanding Music: Genres, Instruments, and Musicians	13
Activities to Discover Individual Musical Tastes and Interests	15
2. SELECTING YOUR INSTRUMENT	17
Brief Description and History of Various Musical Instruments	17
Factors to Consider When Choosing an Instrument	19
Self-assessment Activity to Help with the Decision	20
3. THE ABCS OF MUSIC THEORY	23
Introduction to Basic Music Theory: Notes, Scales, Chords, and Rhythms	23
Simple Activities to Practice These Concepts	25
4. YOUR FIRST MUSIC LESSONS	27
What to Expect From Your First Lessons: How to Prepare and What to Bring	27
The Role of a Music Teacher and How to Work Effectively with Them	29
5. PRACTICING MAKES PERFECT	31
Importance and Benefits of Regular Practice	31
Developing an Effective Practice Routine	33
Developing an Effective Practice Routine	35
6. THE ART OF PERFORMANCE	37
Basics of Performing: From Preparation to Execution	37
Managing Stage Fright	39
Tips for Successful Performances	40
7. JOINING ENSEMBLES AND BANDS	43
The Benefits of Playing Music with Others	43
How to Join a School Band, Orchestra, or Ensemble	44

8. MUSIC COMPETITIONS AND EXAMINATIONS	47
Overview of Various Music Competitions and Exams	47
How to Prepare for These Events and Use Them to Improve	49
9. EXPLORING DIFFERENT MUSIC CAREERS	53
Detailed Look at Various Career Paths in Music: Performing, Teaching, Composing, and More	53
Interviews with Professionals in these Fields	55
10. BUILDING YOUR PRESENCE	59
Introduction to Self-Promotion: Social Media, Websites, and Performances	59
Basic Guide to Recording and Sharing Your Music	61
11. MUSIC AND EDUCATION	63
The Importance of Balancing Music with School	63
Possibilities for Studying Music in Higher Education	65
12. THE PROFESSIONAL WORLD OF MUSIC	67
Explanation of the Music Industry and How It Operates	67
Potential Paths to Becoming a Professional Musician	69
13. OVERCOMING OBSTACLES	71
Conclusion: Your Unique Music Journey	75
Appendices	77

introduction

Hey there, future music star! It's fantastic to see your interest in this fascinating, thrilling, and, most importantly, harmonious journey toward becoming a professional musician. I'm excited to take you on this adventure where you'll uncover the secrets of music, tune your skills, and explore the wondrous world of melodies and high notes. This chapter is all about giving you a sneak peek into what lies ahead in our musical journey together. It's kind of like the exciting intro you hear at the start of a new song, giving you an idea of what to expect.

Have you ever wondered what makes a professional musician? We've all seen them—on TV, on stage, even on our own devices—pouring their heart and soul into their music, making us laugh, cry, dance, or sing along. In this book, we will delve deep into what it takes to join those ranks, to reach the level where your music can move and inspire others just the same. Sounds pretty cool, doesn't it?

But hold your horses! Before you sprint off towards your first Grammy award, remember that all amazing journeys begin with a single step. It's the same with music. We'll start by exploring your personal musical interests and helping you choose an instrument that sings to your heart. Whether it's the

Introduction

soulful strumming of a guitar, the cheerful tinkling of a piano, or the powerful boom of a drum set, we'll figure out together what stirs your musical spirit.

Once we've discovered your instrument of choice, we'll get familiar with the magical world of music theory. But wait! Don't let that term scare you away. Think of music theory as a treasure map. It shows you the path from one musical idea to another, revealing all the exciting connections along the way. And we promise, we'll make it fun and engaging, with plenty of activities to keep you on your toes.

After that, we'll dive headfirst into the art of playing your chosen instrument. We'll go over what to expect from your first lessons and how to make the most of them. And remember, nobody becomes a rockstar in a day. It's all about practice, and this book will share some valuable tips and tricks to make your practice sessions as productive as possible.

But playing music isn't just about practice; it's also about performance. This book will guide you through the exhilarating experience of sharing your music with others, whether it's your parents, friends, or an audience of hundreds at a school talent show.

Music isn't meant to be a solitary journey, though. It's about harmony and synchrony, and what better way to experience that than by joining a band or ensemble? We'll show you the ropes and tell you what to expect when you step into the exciting world of group performances.

And there's more! We will talk about music competitions and examinations—don't worry, they're not as scary as they sound. In fact, they're wonderful opportunities for you to grow as a musician and test your skills. This book will help you navigate these with confidence and grace.

Finally, we'll journey together into the professional world of music. We'll explore the different career paths you can take and meet some amazing people who've turned their passion for music into their job. Plus, we'll also dive into the practical side of things, like building your presence and balancing music with your education.

Phew! That's quite a lot, isn't it? Don't worry. We'll take it one step at a time, one note at a time. And remember, this journey is yours. Everyone's music story is unique, and this book is here to guide you on your path, not dictate your steps.

Are you ready to embark on this thrilling voyage towards becoming a professional musician? If the answer is a resounding 'Yes', then buckle up, grab your instrument of choice, and let's set off on this harmonious adventure together! We're so excited to see where this journey takes you and can't wait to share in the fun, challenges, and victories along the way. Let's make some music!

definition of a professional musician

We're about to embark on a journey, a symphony of sorts, where you'll discover the ins and outs of becoming a professional musician. But before we get to those high notes and crescendos, let's understand what a 'professional musician' really means.

Think about your favorite musicians for a moment. Why do you admire them? Is it the way they strum their guitar, or how they hit those high notes, or perhaps the way they command a crowd? These are all parts of what makes them professional musicians. But the term 'professional musician' goes beyond just being good at playing an instrument or singing a song. It's about commitment, passion, discipline, and a whole lot more!

First and foremost, a professional musician is someone who creates or performs music as their primary occupation. That means music isn't just a hobby or a side gig for them - it's their main job. They dedicate most of their time to creating, practicing, and performing music, just like how a professional athlete spends their time training and competing in their sport.

Introduction

But wait a minute, you might think. Does that mean they play music all day, every day? Not exactly. Being a professional musician involves a whole lot more than just playing music. They compose songs, rehearse with bands or orchestras, record in studios, perform at concerts, and sometimes even teach music to others. It's a whole kaleidoscope of musical activities!

However, playing or singing beautifully isn't enough to become a professional musician. It takes years of practice, dedication, and learning to hone their skills. Just like you wouldn't expect to solve a complex math problem without learning the basics first, musicians also start by learning the fundamentals of music and their chosen instrument. This usually involves music lessons, plenty of practice, and even music exams to test their skills.

And speaking of practice, did you know that professional musicians often practice for several hours a day? It's this dedication and commitment that allows them to master their instrument and continually improve their skills. Whether they're learning a new piece of music, preparing for a performance, or simply wanting to get better, practice is a constant part of a professional musician's life.

Beyond the world of notes and scales, professional musicians also have a keen understanding of music theory. This includes knowing how to read and write sheet music, understanding how melodies and harmonies work together, and even being able to compose their own music. They are like detectives, decoding the secrets of music to create beautiful sounds that we all enjoy.

Now, let's not forget one of the most exciting parts of being a professional musician: performing! Whether it's in front of a small crowd at a local venue or on a big stage in front of thousands of fans, professional musicians share their talent and passion with others through their performances. This not only requires excellent musical skills but also confidence and stage presence.

Becoming a professional musician also means learning to navigate the music industry. This can involve everything from signing contracts and recording albums to promoting their music and planning tours. In other words, it's not just about playing music—it's also about understanding the business side of things.

But you know what the best part is? Despite the challenges and hard work, professional musicians get to do something they love every day. They get to express themselves through their music, touch people's hearts, and even inspire others (like you!) to embark on their own musical journeys.

inspiring words about the journey to becoming a professional musician

You've got a spark in your heart and rhythm in your soul, all set to embark on an incredible journey to become a professional musician. Let's take a moment to appreciate the excitement, courage, and passion that brought you here. Remember, no matter where you're starting from, every great musician was once a beginner too!

Imagine for a moment, you're standing on a stage, lights beaming down on you, and a crowd waiting in anticipation. You hold your instrument close, take a deep breath, and play the first note. It's perfect, resonating through the air, making hearts beat in rhythm. This might seem like a distant dream now, but with determination and hard work, it can become your reality.

There's a beautiful quote by Leonard Bernstein that says, "Music can name the unnameable and communicate the unknowable." As you step into the world of music, you're learning a language that goes beyond words, a language that can touch hearts, lift spirits, and bring people together. Isn't it amazing to think that you could have such an impact?

But here's the thing: just like any great adventure, the

Introduction

journey to becoming a professional musician won't always be a smooth ride. There will be high notes and low notes, melodies and discords. There might be times when your fingers ache from too much practice, or when a tune you've been working on just doesn't sound right. It's all part of the process. Every mistake, every challenge is a stepping stone on your path, helping you become a stronger, more skilled musician.

In these moments, remember the words of the great jazz musician Miles Davis, "Do not fear mistakes. There are none." Each stumble, each wrong note, is an opportunity to learn and grow. Don't be too hard on yourself. No one expects you to be perfect, not even the audience. They are there for the music, for the passion, and for the courage you show by standing on that stage.

And that's what truly matters – your love for music. As you practice, learn, and perform, keep this passion burning brightly. Let it be the beat that keeps you going, the melody that lifts your spirits, and the harmony that brings balance in times of discord.

The journey to becoming a professional musician is unique to every individual. It's like composing your own symphony. You decide the tempo, choose the key, and create the melody. You might find inspiration from your favorite musicians, but remember, this is your song. You get to write it in your own unique way.

There's another great quote by Bono, the lead singer of U2, who said, "Music can change the world because it can change people." As you take this journey, know that you are not just learning to play an instrument or sing a song. You're learning to express yourself, to share your feelings, and to connect with others. You're becoming a part of something bigger than yourself.

On this journey, never forget why you started. Maybe it was the thrill of hearing a beautiful melody, or the joy of playing your first note, or the dream of seeing others enjoy your music.

Whatever your reason, let it guide you, inspire you, and keep you motivated.

This journey you're on, it's an adventure like no other. It's a path filled with discoveries, challenges, victories, and plenty of music. And guess what? You've already taken the first step. You're already on your way.

1 /
uncovering your musical interest

understanding music: genres, instruments, and musicians

HELLO AGAIN, my musical explorer! Ready to dive deeper into the grand ocean of music? This time, we'll be exploring the colourful fish that are the genres, the vibrant corals that are the instruments, and the diverse marine life that represents the musicians. Strap on your scuba gear, and let's start our underwater adventure!

When we talk about genres in music, it's like talking about different types of stories. Just like there are action stories, mystery stories, and fairy tales, there are various genres in music. Each genre has its own unique 'sound' and 'feel'. Some genres might make you want to get up and dance, like pop or hip-hop, while others like classical or jazz might make you want to sit back and let the music wash over you.

You might already have a favorite genre or maybe you enjoy a mix of many. That's the beauty of music! There's something for everyone. As you grow as a musician, you'll start to explore different genres. You might find that you enjoy playing one type of music more than others, and that's completely okay! It's all part of finding your own musical voice.

Next, let's explore the instruments. Instruments are like the characters in a story. Each has its own 'voice' and 'personality'. The piano, for instance, can be soft and sweet, or loud and dramatic. The guitar can sound cool and laid-back or energetic and exciting. And then there's the violin, with its ability to mimic the human voice, creating sounds that are deeply emotional.

Choosing an instrument can be like making a new friend. You might feel an instant connection, or it might take some time to get to know each other. Don't worry if you're unsure about which instrument to pick. This book will guide you through the process, helping you find an instrument that resonates with you.

Finally, we come to the musicians themselves. Just like a coral reef is full of diverse marine life, the world of music is teeming with an array of musicians. From solo artists who captivate audiences with just their voice and a guitar, to orchestras where dozens of musicians come together to create a symphony of sound, the possibilities are endless.

Some musicians choose to master one instrument, while others play multiple instruments. Some write their own music, and others bring to life the compositions of others. There are musicians who prefer the spotlight, while others enjoy being part of a band or orchestra. The point is, there's no 'one size fits all' in music. It's about finding what suits you, what makes your heart sing and your spirit dance.

Remember, every musician, every genre, and every instrument brings something unique to the world of music. They add their own color, creating a vibrant, ever-changing musical landscape. And guess what? You're about to add your own color to this landscape. You're about to become a part of this wonderful world of music.

Just imagine, a few years from now, someone might be listening to a song you've written, or watching a video of you playing an instrument, and they might be inspired to start their

Finding Your Rhythm

own musical journey. Just as you were inspired by your favorite musicians, you too have the power to inspire others.

activities to discover individual musical tastes and interests

Are you ready to go on a treasure hunt? A treasure hunt to discover your unique musical tastes and interests? Perfect! Together, we're going to navigate through a series of fun-filled activities that will help you identify your favorite genres, instruments, and musical styles. This exciting expedition will reveal the treasures of your musical identity!

Activity 1: Musical Bingo

For our first activity, we'll need to create a bingo chart. But instead of numbers, we're going to fill our chart with different genres of music: pop, rock, jazz, country, classical, and many others. Now, every day for the next two weeks, listen to a song or two from a different genre and cross it off your chart. Take notes about what you enjoyed or didn't enjoy about each genre. You might discover a genre you never thought you'd enjoy, or you might find new appreciation for a genre you thought wasn't your style!

Activity 2: Instrument Exploration

Next, we're going to embark on an instrument exploration! Here's what you'll do: watch online videos of people playing different instruments. As you watch, pay attention to how the instrument sounds, how it's played, and how it makes you feel. Take notes on what you liked and didn't like about each instrument. This way, you'll start understanding which instruments 'speak' to you.

Activity 3: The Emotion Evolution

Music is a powerful language of emotions. This activity will help you understand which types of music evoke different emotions in you. Make a playlist of songs from different genres, each associated with a different emotion - happiness, sadness, excitement, calmness, etc. As you listen to each song, note down how it makes you feel. This will help you discover what kinds of music touch your heart and stir your soul.

Activity 4: Be the Critic

This activity is all about expanding your musical horizons. Every week, choose a new album or a set of songs by an artist you're not familiar with. As you listen, imagine you're a music critic. What do you like about the music? What do you dislike? What would you change if you could? This activity will not only help you understand your own musical preferences, but also develop your critical listening skills.

Activity 5: Meet the Musicians

Our last activity involves a bit of research. Choose five musicians - they can be from any genre or era. Learn about their musical journey, their influences, and their styles. As you do this, consider what you admire about each musician. Is it their skill, their creativity, their passion? What can you learn from their journey? This will give you a deeper understanding of the path you're about to take and the footsteps you might follow.

These activities are like your map on this musical treasure hunt. They'll guide you, challenge you, and most importantly, help you discover your own unique musical tastes and interests. But remember, there are no wrong answers or dead-ends on this treasure hunt. This is all about exploration and self-discovery.

Every note you listen to, every instrument you explore, and every musician you learn about is another step on your musical journey. Each activity brings you closer to discovering your musical identity. Who knows, by the end of these activities, you might find yourself humming a new tune, dreaming of a new instrument, or even writing your own song.

2 / selecting your instrument

brief description and history of various musical instruments

ARE you ready to time-travel with me? We're going to embark on a journey through history to meet some of the amazing musical instruments that have helped shape the world of music as we know it. From the strumming strings of the guitar to the resonating keys of the piano, each instrument has a story to tell. So let's tune our time-machines and begin our historical tour!

The Piano

Let's start with the grandeur of the piano. The piano is a versatile instrument, capable of playing both melody and harmony. It's played by striking keys which, in turn, hit hammers that strike strings to produce sound. The piano was invented around 1700 by an Italian named Bartolomeo Cristofori. He wanted to create an instrument that could play both soft and loud sounds – 'piano' means soft, and 'forte' means loud in Italian. Over time, the piano has undergone many changes, but it remains a favourite among musicians worldwide.

The Guitar

Next, we visit the guitar, a popular instrument in many

genres like rock, pop, and blues. The guitar is a stringed instrument that produces sound when the strings are plucked or strummed. The history of the guitar is fascinating! Its ancestors can be traced back over 4000 years to ancient Egypt. The modern guitar, as we know it, took shape in Spain in the 15th century. Over the years, the acoustic guitar has evolved into the electric guitar, opening new horizons in music.

The Violin

Our next stop is the elegant violin. Known for its emotive sound, the violin belongs to the string family. It's played by drawing a bow across the strings or plucking them. The violin was developed in Italy in the early 16th century. Famous violin makers, like Antonio Stradivari, made violins that are considered priceless today. The violin is often associated with classical music, but it's also used in other genres, including folk, country, and even rock!

The Drums

Let's now turn to the rhythm-keeper of the music world: the drums. Drums are part of the percussion family and are played by being struck with sticks or hands. Drums are one of the oldest instruments, with evidence of their existence dating back to 6000 BC! They were used for communication, ceremonies, and of course, music. Today, drums form the backbone of many music styles, keeping the beat and adding energy to the performance.

The Flute

Finally, we'll meet the flute, a member of the woodwind family. Despite its name, modern flutes are typically made of metal. They produce sound when a musician blows air across an opening at one end. Flutes have been around for a very long time, with some ancient flutes made from bird bones and mammoth ivory dating back over 40,000 years! Today, the flute is appreciated for its sweet, melodious sound in orchestras and bands alike.

As we journey through time, exploring the origins and

evolution of these musical instruments, it's astonishing to see how creativity, innovation, and passion for music have shaped their histories. These instruments, each with its unique voice and character, come together to create the symphony of sounds we call music.

factors to consider when choosing an instrument

Ready to embark on an exciting journey to choose your very own instrument? Selecting an instrument is a bit like choosing a new friend. You'll spend a lot of time together, learn from each other, and create fantastic memories. But how do you decide which instrument is right for you? Let's unravel this together.

Factor 1: What Sounds Do You Love?

One of the most important things to consider is what kind of sounds you're drawn to. Do you love the deep, resonant tones of a cello, or are you more attracted to the bright, energetic sounds of a trumpet? Try listening to different types of music and see which instruments' sounds make your heart dance. Remember, you're more likely to practice an instrument if you love the way it sounds!

Factor 2: Size and Physical Comfort

It's important to choose an instrument that is appropriate for your size and physical comfort. For example, a tuba might not be a good choice for a young person because of its size, but a ukulele or a flute could be a perfect fit. Consider the weight of the instrument, how it's held, and if you can comfortably reach all the necessary keys or strings.

Factor 3: Personality Match

Just like people, instruments have different 'personalities'. Some are naturally louder and more energetic, like drums, while others can be quieter and more introspective, like a harp. Think about your personality and consider which instruments might be a good match. If you're outgoing and love being the center of attention, you might enjoy a lead instrument like a guitar. If you prefer to support others and be part of a team, you might love playing a bass guitar in a band.

Factor 4: Practical Considerations

Practical considerations also play a role in choosing an instrument. Think about where and when you'll be practicing. If you're living in an apartment with close neighbors, a quieter instrument like a keyboard with headphones might be a good choice. Consider the cost of the instrument and its maintenance, too. Remember, some instruments require regular servicing or replacement parts, like reeds for a clarinet or new strings for a violin.

Factor 5: Your Musical Goals

What do you dream of doing with your music? If you dream of joining a school band, then a brass instrument like the trumpet could be a perfect choice. If you dream of playing in an orchestra, then maybe the violin is for you. Or if you'd love to write and perform your own songs, then the guitar or piano could be your new best friend.

Choosing an instrument is an exciting adventure, and these factors are your guide. Listen to your heart, consider your options, and remember that this is your musical journey. The instrument you choose is going to be your companion along the way, helping you express your creativity and passion for music.

So, take a deep breath, consider these factors, and embark on your journey to find your instrumental match. It's an exciting moment in your life as a musician. A moment that could spark a lifelong friendship with an instrument, filled with musical exploration and discovery.

self-assessment activity to help with the decision

Now that we've gone through the factors to consider when choosing an instrument, it's time to dive into a fun self-assess-

Finding Your Rhythm

ment activity. This activity will help you reflect on what you've learned, your preferences, and how they can guide you to your perfect instrument. Ready? Grab a piece of paper, a pencil, and let's get started!

Activity 1: Sound Exploration

For this part, you'll need access to a music streaming platform or a music library. Listen to various genres of music, such as classical, jazz, rock, pop, country, or folk. For each genre, note down the instruments that catch your ear. Do you love the warmth of the cello in a symphony, the energetic strum of a guitar in a rock song, or the vibrant beats of drums in a pop song? This exercise will help you understand which sounds you're drawn to.

Activity 2: Size and Comfort Consideration

Remember, comfort and size matter when choosing an instrument. In this section, think about your physical attributes. Do you have long fingers that could easily stretch across piano keys or press down on guitar strings? Are you tall enough to hold a full-sized cello comfortably? Sketch out a list of instruments you are physically comfortable handling.

Activity 3: Personality Match-Up

Instruments have their own personalities, and it's crucial to find one that matches yours. Are you an energetic and loud person who could rock out on drums? Or are you more introspective, perhaps suited for the thoughtful melodies of a piano? Think about your personality traits and write down three instruments that match your character.

Activity 4: Practicalities

Time to think practically. How much space do you have for practicing and storing an instrument? Will loud practices disturb your neighbors or family members? What's your budget for buying and maintaining an instrument? Write down your answers and consider instruments that fit into these constraints.

Activity 5: Dream Board

This is the most fun part! Create a dream board with

pictures or drawings of your musical goals. You could draw yourself playing in a band, performing a solo at a concert, or composing your own music. This visual representation can help you understand your musical ambitions more clearly.

Once you've completed all parts of the activity, it's time to review your notes. Look for patterns and connections. Is there an instrument that keeps popping up in your lists? That might just be the perfect one for you!

Remember, this decision doesn't have to be permanent. Many musicians play multiple instruments or switch their primary instrument over time. This self-assessment is just a starting point on your exciting musical journey.

Choosing your first instrument is like opening a door to a new world of sounds, rhythms, and melodies. It's your personal key to the endless universe of music. And while this decision may seem big, remember: there's no wrong choice. Each instrument offers its unique adventure and learning experience.

3 /
the abcs of music theory

introduction to basic music theory: notes, scales, chords, and rhythms

SO, you're ready to dive into the vast ocean of music theory, are you? Don't worry, we're not going to plunge into the deep end just yet. We'll start at the shallow waters, exploring the four fundamental building blocks of music: notes, scales, chords, and rhythms. Ready to dive in? Let's go!

Notes: The Alphabet of Music

Notes are like the alphabet of music. Just like how we use 26 letters to form all words in English, we use only seven notes to form all music - A, B, C, D, E, F, and G. Each note corresponds to a different pitch. Higher pitches sound like birds chirping, while lower pitches sound like a lion's roar. On most instruments, moving to the right or up usually makes the pitch higher, and moving to the left or down makes the pitch lower.

Scales: The Building Blocks

Now that we know our musical alphabet let's move on to scales. A scale is just a specific pattern of notes. The most common scale in Western music is the major scale, which has a happy and bright sound. The major scale pattern is like a magic staircase: it's always "Whole, Whole, Half, Whole, Whole,

Whole, Half." The "Whole" and "Half" here refer to steps between notes. For example, the C Major scale starts at C and follows the magic staircase: C (start), D (whole step), E (whole step), F (half step), G (whole step), A (whole step), B (whole step), and C (half step).

Chords: Notes in Harmony

A chord is when we play multiple notes together, and they blend harmoniously, like a group of friends singing together. The simplest type of chord is a triad, which consists of three notes. The most common triad is formed by taking the first (root), third, and fifth notes of a scale. For instance, the C major chord includes the notes C, E, and G. Chords form the harmonic backbone of a song and give music its depth and richness.

Rhythms: The Heartbeat of Music

Rhythm is the heartbeat of music. It's what makes you tap your feet or bob your head along with a song. In music, rhythm is all about when notes are played and how long they last. The basic unit of rhythm is the beat, just like the ticking of a clock. Beats are grouped into measures, which are separated by bar lines when written on sheet music. Different notes can take up different amounts of beats, like a whole note (4 beats), a half note (2 beats), or a quarter note (1 beat).

Learning music theory might feel like learning a new language. It might seem a little tricky at first, but remember - every musician starts here. With practice, these concepts will become as familiar to you as your favorite song.

Remember, this is just a first step into the world of music theory. There's so much more to explore, like different types of scales, more complex chords, and intricate rhythms. But for now, congratulations! You've made the first step in understanding the language of music.

Being a musician is like being a music detective. You're learning to decipher the codes of notes, scales, chords, and rhythms. And just like a detective, the more codes you crack,

Finding Your Rhythm

the closer you get to solving the mystery - or in this case, the closer you get to creating beautiful music.

simple activities to practice these concepts

Now that we've covered the basics of music theory, it's time to get hands-on and start practicing. Are you ready for some fun activities that will turn you from a music theory novice into a music theory whiz? Here we go!

Activity 1: Note Naming Game

You can start with a simple note naming game. This activity will help you get familiar with the musical alphabet. Here's how it works: First, print or draw a large musical staff on a piece of paper. Next, grab some small items, like beads or buttons. Assign each item a note name and then ask a friend or family member to place the items on the musical staff. Your job is to name the note correctly. This game is a fantastic way to practice recognizing and naming notes on a music staff!

Activity 2: Scale Scavenger Hunt

Remember how we talked about the "magic staircase" pattern in scales? It's time to go on a scale scavenger hunt. Pick a random note, like E, and try to create an E major scale using the "Whole, Whole, Half, Whole, Whole, Whole, Half" pattern. You can use a piano keyboard or a fretboard diagram if you play the guitar. This activity will help you get the hang of creating major scales.

Activity 3: Chord Construction

For this activity, you'll need some colored pencils or markers. Draw a big circle and divide it into seven sections. Write the notes of a major scale in each section, one note per section. Now, let's build a chord. Highlight the first (root), third, and fifth notes of your scale. There you have it - your first chord! Repeat this activity with different scales to get a feel for chord construction.

Activity 4: Rhythm Clap Back

Rhythm Clap Back is a fantastic way to practice rhythms. You'll need a friend or family member to help. One person claps a rhythm, and the other person has to clap it back. Start with simple rhythms using quarter notes and half notes, and gradually incorporate eighth notes and sixteenth notes as you get more comfortable. This fun game is like a musical version of Simon Says and will help you become more comfortable with different rhythms.

Remember, practice makes perfect, and these activities are designed to help you understand and remember the concepts we've learned about notes, scales, chords, and rhythms.

Take your time with each activity and don't rush through them. The goal isn't to speed through but to understand and absorb. This isn't a race; it's a journey of discovery and learning, full of wonderful sounds, exciting beats, and the joy of music.

Becoming familiar with music theory might seem like a big task, but by breaking it down into fun, manageable activities, it becomes an adventure. Each game and each activity brings you one step closer to understanding the language of music.

You're doing a great job, future virtuosos! Keep practicing, stay curious, and continue exploring the world of music. Before you know it, you'll not only be playing your instrument but understanding the beautiful language of music that resonates in every corner of the world.

4 /
your first music lessons

what to expect from your first lessons: how to prepare and what to bring

YOUR INSTRUMENT HAS BEEN CHOSEN, your excitement is brimming, and your first music lesson is right around the corner. It's normal to feel a mix of excitement and nervousness, but don't worry! This chapter is all about helping you feel ready for that big first day. We'll talk about what to expect, how to prepare, and what to bring to your first music lesson.

What to Expect

Walking into your first music lesson might feel a bit like stepping into a brand-new world. The first thing to remember is that every professional musician once sat where you're sitting – at the start of their musical journey.

Your teacher will be a guide for you in this new world. They might start with some warm-up activities to get to know you and your musical background. Don't worry if you feel like you don't know much yet - that's why you're there, to learn!

Then, they might introduce the instrument to you. They'll talk about different parts of the instrument and how to handle it correctly. This might seem basic, but it's super important. Just like how a knight needs to know his sword, a musician needs to know their instrument.

How to Prepare

Preparing for your first music lesson is all about getting into the right mindset. Think of yourself as an explorer ready for an exciting new adventure. Here are some steps to help you prepare:

* Be Curious: Come ready with questions! If something is confusing or intriguing, don't hesitate to ask. Remember, there are no silly questions in learning.

* Rest Well: Get a good night's sleep before your lesson so you're fresh and ready to absorb new information.

* Practice Listening: Spend some time listening to music that features your chosen instrument. This will help train your ear and get you excited about what you'll be learning.

What to Bring

Now, for the practical bit - what to bring. Here are some essentials:

* Your Instrument: If it's small enough, like a flute or violin, you'll probably be expected to bring your own. Larger instruments like pianos or drum sets will likely be at the lesson location.

* A Notebook and Pen: It's a great idea to jot down what you learn during your lessons. This way, you can look back and review during the week.

* Water Bottle: Staying hydrated is key, especially if you're singing or playing a wind instrument.

* A Folder or Binder: This is to keep any sheet music or handouts your teacher might give you. Staying organized will help you focus on learning instead of looking for lost papers.

* A Positive Attitude: This is the most important thing to bring. Be patient with yourself and remember that learning something new takes time. You're not going to become Beethoven or Billie Eilish in one lesson, and that's okay!

Your first music lesson is an exciting step on your musical

journey. You'll likely learn a lot, maybe even play a few simple notes or beats, and hopefully, have a lot of fun.

the role of a music teacher and how to work effectively with them

Are you ready to dive into the heart of your musical journey? In this chapter, we're going to talk about an essential figure in your adventure – the music teacher. Your teacher is not just someone who knows a lot about music; they are also your guide, mentor, and cheering squad, all rolled into one. Let's explore the role of a music teacher and how you can work effectively with them.

The Role of a Music Teacher

Music teachers are like magicians with a special set of skills. Their magic wand is their deep understanding of music, and their magic spells are the ways they inspire and instruct you. Here's what a music teacher does:

* Instructor: Your music teacher will teach you how to play your chosen instrument, understand music theory, and interpret sheet music. They will guide you through the techniques, dynamics, and styles that form the foundation of your musical knowledge.

* Mentor: A music teacher is more than just an instructor; they're also a mentor. They will inspire you, challenge you, and push you to achieve your best. They'll share stories about their own experiences and the journey they've taken in music, providing valuable life lessons along the way.

* Cheerleader: When you hit the right notes, your teacher will be there to cheer you on. And when you stumble, they'll be there to encourage you, reminding you that mistakes are just opportunities for learning.

Working Effectively with Your Music Teacher

Just like in any relationship, your bond with your music teacher is a two-way street. Here's how you can do your part to make it a fruitful journey:

* Communicate Openly: If you have questions, ask! If you're struggling with something, say it. Your teacher can't read your mind. The more you communicate, the better they can help you.

* Practice Regularly: Your music teacher will give you tasks or exercises to do at home. Make sure to practice them. Remember, your growth as a musician doesn't just happen in the classroom. It's also about the time and effort you put in when you're alone with your instrument.

* Respect Your Teacher's Time: Be punctual for your lessons. If you have to cancel, do so in advance. Your teacher's time is valuable, and showing respect for it will help build a good relationship.

* Be Open to Feedback: Your teacher's job is to help you improve, and that means pointing out where you can do better. Don't take it personally. Instead, see it as a gift that will help you become a better musician.

* Stay Curious: Show enthusiasm for learning. Try exploring different types of music or asking your teacher about their favorite composers or musicians. Your curiosity will fuel your learning and make your lessons more interesting for both of you.

Your relationship with your music teacher is a special one. Together, you'll explore the world of music, experience the highs and lows of learning, and celebrate your progress.

5 /
practicing makes perfect

importance and benefits of regular practice

WE'RE GOING to dive into a crucial part of your musical journey – practicing. I know, I know, practice might not sound as thrilling as playing a concert or jamming with a band, but let me assure you, it's like the secret sauce of music. And I'm going to let you in on that secret. So, let's get ready to explore the importance and benefits of regular practice.

Why Is Practice Important?

Imagine you're a brave adventurer setting out on a quest, equipped with a magical instrument. Your goal? To unlock the instrument's magical powers (aka beautiful music!). Now, how do you suppose you'll uncover these hidden melodies and harmonies? That's right! By getting to know your instrument, trying different techniques, and yes, through lots of practice.

Just like learning to ride a bike or mastering a video game level, becoming proficient at a musical instrument takes time and repetition. Every time you sit down to practice, you're strengthening the connection between your brain and your hands or voice, making it easier to hit the right notes or maintain the right rhythm.

Benefits of Regular Practice

Practicing regularly has some incredible perks. Here are a few of the superpowers you can gain from it:

* Improvement in Skill: This one's a no-brainer. The more you practice, the better you get. Your fingers will learn where to go, your voice will hit the right pitches, and you'll start to play more fluently.

* Increased Confidence: As you improve, you'll feel more confident. Not just in your musical abilities, but overall. Completing a difficult piece or mastering a tricky rhythm is incredibly satisfying, and that feeling of accomplishment boosts your self-esteem.

* Better Memory: Believe it or not, regular practice can actually help improve your memory. This is because playing music requires you to remember patterns, sequences, and structures.

* Enhanced Focus and Discipline: Sitting down to practice regularly teaches you focus and discipline. These are valuable skills that can help you in school and other parts of your life too.

* Express Yourself: Regular practice helps you express your emotions through music. You'll begin to understand how different notes, chords, or rhythms can convey different feelings, giving you a new language to express yourself.

Making Practice Fun and Effective

Now, you might be thinking, "Okay, practice is important, but how do I make it fun?" Here are a few tips to keep your practice sessions interesting and productive:

* Set Goals: Setting small, achievable goals for each practice session gives you something to aim for. It could be mastering a few bars of a difficult piece or perfecting a particular rhythm.

* Mix It Up: Practice different things. Work on a variety of skills – scales, chords, songs. This will not only make your practice time more interesting but also make you a more versatile musician.

* Take Breaks: Don't try to cram all your practice into one long session. Take short breaks to rest and recharge. This will

keep you from getting too tired or frustrated and help you focus better when you're practicing.

* Celebrate Progress: Celebrate your achievements, no matter how small. Mastered that difficult chord? Played that tricky piece without a mistake? Give yourself a pat on the back. It's important to acknowledge and enjoy your progress.

Practicing might seem like a daunting task, but it's really just a series of small steps that lead to great music. As you become more comfortable with your instrument and start to see improvement, you might just find that practice isn't a chore, but a joy.

developing an effective practice routine

Ready to put your new superpower, practicing, into action? Great! Because this chapter is all about creating an effective practice routine. Think of it like a game plan, a strategy that'll help you get the most out of your practice time. Ready to learn the secrets to a super-charged practice routine? Let's dive in!

What's a Practice Routine?

A practice routine is a plan that outlines what you will work on during your practice sessions. It includes things like scales, exercises, pieces you're learning, and even fun music activities. Having a routine helps you stay organized and focused, and makes sure that you're giving time and attention to all the important aspects of your music learning.

Creating Your Practice Routine

So, how do you create your own practice routine? Here are some steps to guide you:

1. Decide on the Duration: How long can you practice each day? It could be 30 minutes, an hour, or even longer. What's important is that you choose a length of time that's realistic for you.

2. Split Your Time: Divide your practice time into different sections. For example, you might spend the first 10 minutes on

warm-up exercises, the next 20 minutes on scales and technical work, the next 20 minutes on a piece you're learning, and the last 10 minutes on music you enjoy playing or exploring new songs.

3. Set Goals: For each section of your practice, set a specific goal. This could be something like, "Play the C Major scale smoothly" or "Learn the first line of my new piece."

4. Be Flexible: Some days you might want to spend more time on a piece that's giving you trouble, or you might feel like playing your favorite music for a bit longer. That's perfectly fine. Your routine is there to guide you, not to restrict you.

Tips for an Effective Practice Routine

Now, let's look at some tips that'll help you supercharge your practice routine:

* Consistency is Key: Practice regularly, ideally at the same time each day. This helps to create a habit. Your brain will start to expect that it's time to practice, and it'll be easier to get into the flow of practicing.

* Warm Up: Start your practice with some warm-up exercises. These help to prepare your fingers or your voice for the session ahead.

* Slow and Steady: When you're learning a new piece or a difficult part of a song, practice slowly at first. This helps your brain and your muscles learn what they need to do. As you get more comfortable, you can gradually increase the speed.

* Cool Down: Just like with sports, it's important to cool down after a practice session. You could do this by playing a piece you know well, or simply by taking a few moments to relax and breathe deeply.

* Make It Fun: Remember to include music you enjoy in your practice routine. This will help keep you motivated and make your practice sessions something you look forward to.

There you have it, the blueprint for your own super-charged practice routine. Creating a routine might take a little bit of time and thought, but the benefits you'll gain will be well worth it.

So, pick up your instrument, set your goals, and let the rhythm of your practice routine guide you on your journey to musical greatness.

developing an effective practice routine

Are you ready to power up your music journey? You're about to discover the secret weapon every successful musician has in their toolkit: an effective practice routine. This chapter is your guide to creating a routine that will help you shine brightly in your musical journey. Let's get started!

Practice Routine: Your Musical Map

Imagine going on an exciting treasure hunt without a map. Tricky, right? A practice routine is your map in the world of music, guiding you through what to focus on during your practice sessions. It's like having your own personalized plan for success!

Crafting Your Personal Practice Routine

So, how do we build this magical map? Let's break it down into four easy steps:

1. Time Allocation: First, decide how much time you can dedicate to practice each day. It could be half an hour, one hour, or even more. Remember, the key is consistent daily practice.

2. Break It Down: Divide your practice time into various sections. You could begin with warm-up exercises, then work on scales and technical drills, move on to pieces you're learning, and end with playing songs you love or experimenting with new tunes.

3. Set Clear Goals: For each section, have a clear goal. Whether it's "Master the G Major scale" or "Play the first eight bars of my new piece without mistakes", having clear objectives will give your practice purpose.

4. Stay Flexible: This routine isn't set in stone. Some days you might want to spend more time on a tricky song or take extra time for fun music exploration. That's totally okay!

Supercharging Your Practice Routine: Top Tips

Now, let's look at some strategies to make your practice routine super effective:

* Consistency Counts: Practice at the same time every day, creating a regular habit. Your brain will recognize this pattern, making it easier to dive into the music zone.

* Begin with a Warm-Up: Just like athletes, musicians need to warm up. Start with simple exercises to get your fingers or voice ready.

* Patience Pays Off: When learning new songs or difficult parts, start slow. Let your brain and muscles get used to the movements, and gradually increase the speed as you become more comfortable.

* Time to Cool Down: After an intense practice session, a cool-down phase is crucial. This could involve playing a piece you're familiar with or taking a few minutes to relax and breathe.

* Keep the Fun Factor: Don't forget to include music you enjoy playing. Keeping the fun alive will help you stay motivated and make practice something you look forward to.

And there you have it! You now have all the tools to create a practice routine that's perfectly tailored to you. Remember, developing a good practice routine may take a little time and effort, but the rewards will be amazing. Each note you play, each rhythm you master, and each song you learn is a step closer to your dream of becoming a professional musician.

6 / the art of performance

basics of performing: from preparation to execution

NOW, let's talk about something truly exciting - performing! Performing isn't just about playing music; it's about sharing your musical journey with others. It can seem a bit nerve-wracking at first, but don't worry. We'll walk through this together, from the preparation stages to the actual performance. Ready? Let's get started!

1. Preparation is Key

You know the saying, "Practice makes perfect?" Well, it's especially true for performances. The better you know your piece, the more confident you'll feel on stage. Dedicate time each day to practice the pieces you'll perform, and try to memorize them if possible. This way, even if you get a bit nervous during the performance, your hands will know what to do!

2. The Dress Rehearsal

Before the actual performance, it's a great idea to have a dress rehearsal, which is basically a practice performance. You can do this in your living room or any other space where you feel comfortable. Dress up as if it's the real performance, invite your family or friends, and perform your piece just like you would on the big day. This will help you feel more prepared and less nervous when the time comes.

3. Setting the Stage

Imagine walking out onto the stage. There are bright lights, and the audience is waiting for you to begin. It might seem scary, but think of it this way: the audience is there because they want to hear your music. They are excited to see you perform!

4. Dealing with Stage Fright

Almost everyone feels nervous before a performance. Even famous musicians admit they still get butterflies in their stomachs before they go on stage. The trick is to use that nervous energy to your advantage. Think of it as excitement, not fear. Take a few deep breaths before you start, and remind yourself that you're there to share your music, something you love.

5. The Performance

Now, it's time for the performance. Walk confidently onto the stage, smile at the audience, and then lose yourself in the music. Remember, you're not just playing notes; you're telling a story with your music. If you make a mistake, don't panic. Just keep going. Most of the time, the audience won't even notice.

6. Connecting with the Audience

of performing is connecting with your audience. Look up from your instrument occasionally and make eye contact with the audience. This shows them you're engaged and excited to share your music with them. After all, a performance is a conversation between you and the audience, told through the language of music.

7. The Grand Finale

When you reach the end of your performance, hold your last note for a moment, then let your hands fall away from your instrument. Take a deep breath, smile, and stand up to take a bow. You did it!

8. Reflecting on the Performance

After the performance, take some time to reflect. What went

well? What could you improve for next time? Remember, every performance is a learning opportunity.

managing stage fright

Today, we're diving into a topic that even the most experienced musicians grapple with - stage fright. Feeling nervous before a performance is completely natural, but we have some tips and tricks that can help you conquer those butterflies in your stomach. Are you ready? Let's dive in!

1. Understanding Stage Fright

First things first, let's understand what stage fright is. It's a type of anxiety that can affect anyone who needs to perform in front of others. Even though it's called "stage" fright, it can happen in any situation where you feel the spotlight is on you. It's perfectly normal to feel a bit nervous when all eyes are on you, but remember, the audience is rooting for you, not against you.

2. Mind Over Matter

Your mind is a powerful tool. Try visualizing your performance. Close your eyes and imagine yourself on stage, playing your piece perfectly from start to finish. Hear the applause of the audience in your mind. Practicing this kind of positive visualization can help you feel more confident and less anxious.

3. The Power of Practice

We can't emphasize enough how important practice is! The more familiar you are with your music, the less likely you are to get flustered if you make a mistake. Also, practicing in front of others, such as family members or friends, can help you get used to the idea of performing.

4. Breathing Exercises

One of the simplest and most effective ways to calm your nerves is to focus on your breathing. Try taking slow, deep breaths before you go on stage. This can help to lower your heart rate and help you feel more calm and centered.

5. The Importance of Warm-ups

Just like athletes warm up before a big game, musicians need to warm up before a performance too. Playing some scales or doing finger exercises can help to loosen up your fingers and your mind. Plus, it can serve as a reminder that you know what you're doing.

6. The Buddy System

Having someone with you backstage can be a great comfort. This person could be a fellow performer, a teacher, or a family member. They can help to distract you, offer words of encouragement, or just provide a familiar face in the crowd.

7. Self-Care Matters

Taking care of your overall health can also help manage stage fright. Make sure to eat a good meal before your performance, stay hydrated, and get a good night's sleep. You'll feel more prepared and energized.

8. Embrace the Nerves

Finally, remember that it's okay to be nervous. In fact, some performers believe that a little bit of nerves can actually improve your performance by giving you an extra burst of energy and focus. So, rather than trying to eliminate your nerves entirely, try to embrace them.

9. Learn from Experience

Each performance is an opportunity to grow and learn. After your performance, reflect on what you did well and what you could improve on for next time.

tips for successful performances

Now that we've tackled stage fright, let's talk about the fun part - your actual performance. How can you make it the best it can be? Here are some top-notch tips to guide you along the way.

1. Know Your Music Inside Out

This might sound obvious, but the better you know your music, the better your performance will be. Spend ample time

Finding Your Rhythm

practicing until you can play your piece effortlessly. Knowing your music well also allows you to recover quickly if a mistake happens during your performance.

2. Connect with Your Music

A key to a great performance is to not just play the notes, but to connect with the music emotionally. Try to understand the mood of the piece you're performing. Is it joyful, melancholy, or dramatic? Expressing the emotion of the music can make your performance more engaging for the audience.

3. Dress the Part

What you wear can make a big difference. Dress appropriately for the venue and occasion. Not only will it make you look professional, but it also shows respect for the audience and for the music.

4. Warm Up Before Performing

As we mentioned in the last chapter, warming up is essential. It helps prepare both your mind and body for the performance. Play some scales, do some stretches, or perform parts of your piece that are particularly challenging.

5. Respect Your Audience

Always remember to show your appreciation for the audience. They've taken the time to come and listen to you. So, a simple bow or verbal thank you can go a long way.

6. Take Your Time

Once you're on stage, take a moment to settle yourself. Adjust your instrument, take a deep breath, and then start when you're ready. There's no need to rush.

7. Maintain a Good Posture

Good posture isn't just important for your health; it also affects your performance. Sit or stand straight, hold your instrument correctly, and stay relaxed. This helps you breathe better, play better, and look more confident.

8. Keep Going

In the event of a mistake during a performance, keep going. Most of the time, your audience won't even notice a small error unless you draw attention to it by stopping or reacting.

9. Enjoy the Moment

Lastly, remember to enjoy yourself. Yes, you're there to impress the audience with your skills, but music is also about joy and expression. If you enjoy what you're doing, your audience will likely enjoy it too.

7 / joining ensembles and bands

the benefits of playing music with others

HEY MUSICAL WIZARDS! By now, you've had a taste of what it's like to work on music solo, but have you thought about the magic that can happen when you play music with others? Let's dive into the wonderful world of group music-making.

1. Learning to Listen

When you play music with others, one of the first things you'll learn is how to listen. You'll need to pay attention to what your fellow musicians are playing and how it blends with your own part. This will not only make you a better musician but also a more sensitive listener, which is a great skill in everyday life.

2. Improving Your Timing

Playing in a group requires you to keep time with other musicians. You'll have to stay in rhythm and match the speed of the group. This can improve your sense of timing, which is crucial to any good performance.

3. Developing Teamwork

Making music in a group is all about teamwork. You'll learn to work together, respect each other's parts, and adjust to make the best possible sound. This experience can help you develop great teamwork skills that can be useful in all areas of life.

4. Gaining Different Perspectives

Each musician has their own unique way of interpreting music. By playing with others, you can learn from their perspectives, broaden your musical understanding, and enrich your own interpretation.

5. Boosting Confidence

Performing with others can also boost your confidence. There's a certain comfort in knowing that you're not alone on stage, which can help you feel more confident and less nervous. Plus, seeing your fellow musicians perform confidently can inspire you to do the same.

6. Expanding Your Musical Repertoire

Different people often have different tastes in music. By playing with others, you'll get exposed to a wider variety of music than you might on your own. This can expand your musical repertoire and expose you to new styles and genres.

7. Creating a Sense of Community

Music has a way of bringing people together. When you play music with others, you share in a common goal and create something beautiful together. This can foster a sense of community and belonging.

8. Having Fun

Last, but certainly not least, playing music with others is just plain fun! It's a way to express yourself, make new friends, and create joyful memories.

how to join a school band, orchestra, or ensemble

Now that we've discussed the magic of playing music with others, it's time to discover how you can join a school band, orchestra, or ensemble. Let's take a look at some steps that might help you find your spot in one of these exciting musical groups!

1. Discovering Your Options

Your first task is to find out what musical groups are available at your school. This might include a band, orchestra, jazz ensemble, or even a choir. Your school's website or music department will likely have this information. If not, ask your music teacher or school counselor for help.

2. Choosing the Right Group for You

Each musical group will have its unique requirements and characteristics. An orchestra mainly comprises string instruments, while a band includes brass, woodwind, and percussion instruments. A jazz ensemble might require different skills, like improvisation. Find out as much as you can about each group and consider which one fits your interests and abilities.

3. Understanding the Audition Process

Many musical groups require you to audition. An audition is a short performance where you demonstrate your skills. Find out what you need to prepare for your audition. This might include playing a certain piece of music, demonstrating scales, or even sight-reading. Remember, auditions aren't meant to be scary. They're just a way for the director to understand your current skills and see how you might fit into the group.

4. Preparing for Your Audition

Once you know what's required for the audition, start preparing. Practice the required piece of music, and work on any additional skills you'll need to demonstrate. If you're feeling nervous, remember that practice is the best way to build confidence. And don't forget to ask your music teacher for help if you're feeling stuck or unsure.

5. The Audition Day

On the day of the audition, arrive early and give yourself time to warm up. Bring any necessary materials, such as sheet music or your instrument. Remember to breathe, take your time, and show your love for music. Even if you make a mistake, keep going. Directors are looking for potential and passion, not perfection!

6. Awaiting the Results

After the audition, you'll usually have to wait for the results. Try to stay patient, and remember that no matter the outcome, you've taken a courageous step. Not making it this time doesn't mean you're not talented. It just means you have more opportunities to grow and learn.

7. If You're Selected

Congratulations! If you've been selected to join a group, there will likely be a meeting to discuss schedules, expectations, and other details. Make sure to attend and ask any questions you might have. Remember, joining a musical group is a commitment, and you'll be expected to attend practices and performances regularly.

8. If You're Not Selected

Don't be disheartened if you're not selected this time. Use this experience as a learning opportunity. Ask for feedback, and use it to improve your skills. Keep practicing and try again next time. Your journey in music is filled with both challenges and victories, each one making you a stronger musician.

Being part of a school band, orchestra, or ensemble can provide you with valuable musical experiences. It will allow you to make music with others, learn to work in a team, and improve your musical skills. So, don't be afraid to take this leap and add another exciting chapter to your musical journey. You've got this, and remember, the world is waiting to hear your music!

8 /
music competitions and examinations

overview of various music competitions and exams

NOW THAT YOU'RE well on your way to becoming part of a musical ensemble, let's explore another important aspect of a young musician's journey – music competitions and exams. These can provide valuable learning experiences and opportunities to showcase your talent.

1. What are Music Competitions?

Music competitions are events where musicians perform and compete against each other. They come in all shapes and sizes, from small local events to grand international competitions. You could compete as a solo musician, as part of a duo, or even with your school band or orchestra. The best part? They're an excellent chance to share your music, learn from other musicians, and sometimes even win prizes!

2. Different Types of Music Competitions

There are many kinds of music competitions. Some focus on specific instruments like piano or violin, others might be about singing or songwriting, and some even cater to specific genres like classical or jazz. Research online or ask your music teacher about competitions that suit your interests and skills.

3. Preparing for a Music Competition

Competitions often require you to prepare specific pieces of music. Just like for your school band audition, practice is the key. Rehearse your piece until you feel confident, but also remember to keep it enjoyable. Music is about expressing yourself and having fun!

4. What are Music Exams?

Music exams are different from competitions. Instead of competing against others, you're showcasing your skills to a panel of examiners who will assess your performance. In many ways, music exams are like a report card for your musical progress.

5. Different Types of Music Exams

There are various organizations that offer music exams, like the Associated Board of the Royal Schools of Music (ABRSM) or Trinity College London. These exams usually consist of performance pieces, scales, sight-reading, and sometimes aural tests or music theory. Each level of the exam gets progressively more challenging, allowing you to continuously expand your musical skills.

6. Preparing for a Music Exam

Just like with competitions, the best way to prepare for an exam is to practice. Your music teacher can help you select pieces and prepare the required skills. It might feel a bit stressful at times, but remember that it's all part of your musical journey.

7. The Benefits of Competitions and Exams

You might be wondering, "Why would I want to compete or take an exam?" Well, both can provide valuable feedback on your performance and help you set goals. They also offer chances to perform in front of an audience, which is an important skill for any musician.

8. Balance is Key

While competitions and exams can be beneficial, it's also important to maintain a balance. Music is about joy and expression, not just winning or getting good grades. Make sure to spend time playing music just for fun, too!

9. The Power of Persistence

Competitions and exams may sometimes be challenging, and there might be times when you don't win or get the grade you hoped for. That's perfectly okay! Every musician, even famous ones, face setbacks. What matters is that you keep going, keep learning, and keep enjoying your music.

Music competitions and exams are just another part of your exciting journey as a budding musician. They offer opportunities to shine, learn, and grow. However, remember that your worth as a musician is not defined by the awards you win or the grades you receive. What truly matters is the passion, creativity, and enjoyment you bring to your music.

how to prepare for these events and use them to improve

How's the musical journey going? Now that we've covered what music competitions and exams are all about, let's move on to something even more exciting – preparing for these events and using them to sharpen your skills and enhance your love for music. Excited? Let's hit the right notes together!

1. Choosing the Right Event

Before you begin preparing, it's important to select the right event for you. Remember, the aim is to enjoy and learn, not to overwhelm yourself. Chat with your music teacher about what kind of competition or exam might suit you best. Think about what instrument you want to focus on, what kind of music you love to play, and where your strengths lie.

2. Setting Goals

Every music event is a chance to grow. Maybe you want to get better at sight-reading, or perhaps you want to boost your confidence on stage. Set specific goals for each event to guide your preparation and focus your efforts.

3. Developing a Practice Routine

Your practice routine is the foundation of your preparation. Be consistent and patient. Learning music isn't about rushing to the finish line; it's about enjoying every step of the journey. Start by breaking your practice time into sections. You could spend some time on scales, then work on your competition pieces, and wrap up with some sight-reading or improvisation. Make sure to also include plenty of breaks!

4. Staying Healthy and Fit

Just like athletes need to keep their bodies in shape for a race, musicians need to keep their bodies and minds in top shape for performances. Make sure you're getting enough rest, eating healthily, and taking care of your mental well-being. And don't forget about your posture! Good posture can help prevent injury and make your practice sessions more comfortable.

5. Learning from the Experience

After every competition or exam, take some time to reflect. How did you feel during the performance? What went well, and what could you improve? Use this experience as a learning opportunity. Remember, it's not just about the result, but about the journey and what you learn along the way.

6. Handling Nerves

Feeling nervous before a performance is normal. But remember, nerves can actually help you perform better! They can make you more alert and energized. To help manage your nerves, try techniques like deep breathing, visualization, or even doing a bit of light exercise before your performance.

7. Celebrating Your Achievements

After your performance, give yourself a pat on the back. You've worked hard, and you deserve to be proud of yourself, no matter the outcome. Celebrate your achievement with your friends, family, or music teacher. Remember, every performance is an accomplishment in itself!

8. Remember Why You Play

As you prepare for music events, remember why you love

playing music. Is it the beautiful sounds you create, the stories you can tell, or simply the fun of playing your favorite songs? Keep this reason at the heart of your preparation. This love for music will shine through in your performances and help you through the hard times.

Music competitions and exams are wonderful adventures on your journey as a young musician. They provide opportunities for growth, learning, and sharing your music with others. So, take a deep breath, hold your instrument high, and step onto the stage of your musical journey with confidence and joy.

9 /
exploring different music careers

detailed look at various career paths in music: performing, teaching, composing, and more

READY FOR ANOTHER EXCITING JOURNEY? You've been playing, practicing, and performing, but have you ever thought about what it would be like to make music your career? Imagine waking up every day to do something you truly love! In this chapter, we'll explore some of the many career paths in music. Get ready to uncover the wide world of musical professions!

1. Performing

First stop on our journey is the spotlight of the stage – performing! Performers are the rockstars and soloists who captivate audiences with their musical talent. As a performer, you could be playing your favorite melodies in a grand concert hall, jamming out with a band in a cozy café, or even dazzling crowds on the streets with your busking skills! It's a career full of excitement, creativity, and applause.

2. Teaching

Next, we hop off the stage and into the classroom – welcome to the world of music teaching. As a music teacher, you can inspire young minds, just like your music teacher inspires you! You could work in a school, teach private lessons at home, or even guide students online. Teaching music is all about sharing your passion, nurturing talent, and celebrating the joy of music with others.

3. Composing

Ready to create your own unique sound? Welcome to the realm of composing. Composers write new music – from pop songs to symphonies. As a composer, you could write music for movies, video games, orchestras, bands, or even your own solo performances. Composing allows you to express your emotions, tell stories, and invent new musical worlds through your creations.

4. Conducting

Now, let's step onto the podium and pick up the baton – it's time to conduct. Conductors lead orchestras, choirs, or bands, guiding them through musical performances. As a conductor, you would shape the sound of the group, bringing the music to life in your unique way. It's a role that requires leadership, a good ear, and a clear vision of what you want the music to sound like.

5. Music Therapy

Now, let's explore a path where music meets healing – music therapy. Music therapists use the power of music to help people improve their health and wellbeing. You might work in hospitals, schools, or private practices, using music to help people express themselves, improve their motor skills, or even cope with stress and anxiety.

6. Music Production

Are you into technology and sound? Let's dive into the world of music production! Music producers work in studios, helping to record, edit, and mix music. They often work closely with musicians to shape the sound of their recordings. This is a great field for those who love both music and technology.

7. Music Journalism

Finding Your Rhythm

Last but not least, we have music journalism, a career that blends love for music with the written word. As a music journalist, you could write album reviews, interview musicians, or report on music events. You could work for a newspaper, magazine, website, or even start your own music blog!

Remember, Music Explorer, this is just a taste of the many career paths in music. Each path has its own unique rhythms and melodies, and the best part is, you can explore more than one! You might be a performing musician who also teaches or a composer who also conducts. The world of music is vast and exciting, full of opportunities to express yourself, share your love for music, and make a difference in the world.

As we continue our musical journey together, remember that your path in music is yours to choose. Whether you're dreaming of standing on a grand stage, composing your own symphony, or teaching the next generation of musicians, know that every note you play brings you one step closer to your dream.

interviews with professionals in these fields

You've discovered the various career paths in music, and now it's time to hear from some real-life music professionals. We have an exciting line-up of experts ready to share their experiences. Let's get the show on the road!

Interview with Laura, the Concert Pianist

First up, we have Laura, a concert pianist who travels the world playing music.

"Hi, I'm Laura! I started learning the piano when I was five, and now I perform in concert halls around the world. Practice is my best friend! It's not always easy, but the feeling when I play a piece perfectly is absolutely amazing. My advice to young musicians is to never stop exploring new pieces and challenging yourself!"

Interview with Mark, the Music Teacher

Next, let's chat with Mark, a music teacher who works in a middle school.

"Hello, explorers! I'm Mark. I loved music as a kid and now, I love helping kids like you discover their musical talents. The best part of my job? Seeing my students' faces light up when they finally nail a tricky piece of music. If you love sharing your love for music, teaching could be the path for you!"

Interview with Sophia, the Composer

Now, let's meet Sophia, a composer who creates music for video games.

"Hi there! I'm Sophia. I've always loved video games and music, so becoming a video game composer was a dream come true. I create all kinds of music - from epic orchestral pieces to quirky little tunes. My advice to young composers is to listen to all kinds of music and let your imagination run wild!"

Interview with Liam, the Conductor

Let's hear from Liam, a conductor who leads a local community orchestra.

"Greetings! I'm Liam. As a conductor, I get to work with a team of talented musicians to create beautiful performances. It's a lot like being a coach of a sports team. I love the energy of live performances - it's truly electrifying! If you enjoy teamwork and have a keen ear for music, conducting might be for you!"

Interview with Maya, the Music Therapist

Now, we're off to meet Maya, a music therapist who uses music to help people heal.

"Hello, everyone! I'm Maya. I work with people of all ages, using music to help them express their feelings and improve their wellbeing. It's incredibly rewarding to see how music can bring joy and comfort to people. If you want a career that blends music and helping others, consider music therapy!"

Interview with Ethan, the Music Producer

Let's chat with Ethan, a music producer who works in a recording studio.

*"Hey, future musicians! I'm Ethan. I help artists record their

music and make it sound just right. I love the creative process and the satisfaction of hearing the final product. If you're into technology and love shaping sound, check out music production!"*

Interview with Ava, the Music Journalist

Lastly, let's hear from Ava, a music journalist who writes about the latest music trends.

"Hi there, Music Explorers! I'm Ava. I write about new music releases, interview musicians, and attend concerts for my job - it's a lot of fun! If you love music and writing, music journalism might be a great fit for you!"

What a fantastic set of interviews! Each of these professionals found their unique path in the world of music. As we wrap up this chapter, remember that there's no one "right" way to have a career in music. Whether you're on stage or behind the scenes, what matters most is your passion for music.

10 / building your presence

introduction to self-promotion: social media, websites, and performances

WE'VE HAD a chance to delve into the world of music careers and learn from professionals. Now, it's time to turn the spotlight onto you! This chapter is all about how you can put your talent out there for the world to see. Ready to dive in? Let's go!

When you hear the word "self-promotion," you might think it's about showing off. But it's actually more about sharing! It's about letting people know about your music and inviting them to be a part of your journey. It's like sharing a secret treasure with your friends – only in this case, you're sharing your music with the world.

Social Media

Social media is like a digital playground. It's where people from all over the world gather to share their stories, ideas, and talents. And it's a great place for young musicians like you to start sharing your music.

Remember to talk with your parents or guardians before you start using social media. They can help you set up your accounts safely and guide you on using them responsibly.

Platforms like YouTube, Instagram, and TikTok are great

places to share videos of your performances. Facebook, on the other hand, can help you connect with local music groups or bands. Remember, it's not just about posting your content, but also about engaging with your audience. Respond to comments, ask for feedback, and thank your followers for their support.

Websites

Having your own website can be like having a digital home for your music. It's a place where people can go to learn more about you and your musical journey. You can share your performance videos, photos, upcoming events, and even your thoughts about music.

Building a website may sound complicated, but there are many user-friendly platforms like Wix, Squarespace, or WordPress that make it easy and fun. It's like constructing a virtual treehouse, except instead of hammer and nails, you're using images, texts, and links.

Performances

Performances are the beating heart of a musician's life. They're where you get to share your music live and connect directly with your audience. School recitals, local concerts, community events, even online live performances are all great opportunities.

Remember to announce your performances on your social media and website. You can make it exciting with a countdown, or share behind-the-scenes photos of your preparation. This builds anticipation and encourages more people to attend or tune in.

As we wrap up this chapter, remember that self-promotion is all about connecting with others. It's about inviting people into your musical world and making them feel welcome. Be patient and keep sharing, because every great musician starts with a single listener.

basic guide to recording and sharing your music

After learning about promoting your musical journey, we bet you're eager to start creating your own music. And what better way to do that than by learning how to record and share your tunes? Buckle up, because we're diving into the world of recording!

Step 1: Set Up Your Space

First things first, we need to create a good space for recording. Try to find a quiet room with little background noise. Can you hear the neighbor's dog barking? The washing machine rumbling? If yes, it might be a good idea to find a quieter spot.

Next, arrange your space. You'll need a chair, a music stand for your sheet music, your instrument, and of course, a device to record with. A smartphone or a tablet will do just fine for starters. Set up your device on a stable surface, at a distance that captures both you and your instrument.

Step 2: Do a Sound Check

Before you hit record, do a quick sound check. Play a few notes or a part of your song and then listen back to it. Can you hear your instrument clearly? Is the volume just right? If not, adjust your device's distance or your instrument's position until it sounds good.

Step 3: Recording Your Music

Now, you're ready to record! Relax, take a deep breath, and start playing. Remember, it's okay if you make a mistake. You can always pause and start again. The most important thing is to enjoy the process!

When you're done, save your recording and give it a listen. Are you happy with it? If not, don't worry! The beauty of recording is that you can do it as many times as you need until you get it just right.

Step 4: Sharing Your Music

Once you're happy with your recording, it's time to share it!

There are lots of ways to do this. You can send it to your friends or family through messaging apps or email. Or, you can post it on your social media platforms, or your personal music website if you have one.

You could even upload it to music sharing platforms like Soundcloud or Bandcamp. This might be something you want to explore as you get more comfortable with recording. And remember, always discuss with your parents or guardians before sharing anything online.

Step 5: Be Proud and Keep Learning

Congratulations! You've just recorded and shared your music. That's a big achievement! Be proud of yourself, and remember to take a moment to appreciate your hard work.

Keep in mind that recording is a skill that gets better with practice. Your first few recordings might not sound perfect, and that's perfectly okay. With time, you'll learn more about controlling your sound, expressing yourself, and even about editing and improving your recordings.

11 /
music and education

the importance of balancing music with school

I HOPE you've been enjoying your journey into the world of music so far. Today, we'll explore a vital part of your journey – learning to balance your music practice with school.

1: The Double Reward – Music and School

Playing an instrument can be such a joy, can't it? The thrill of learning a new piece, the satisfaction when your fingers finally hit all the right notes - it's truly magical. But there's also school, with its own set of fascinating subjects, homework, and activities. Balancing the two can seem a bit like juggling, but don't worry, it's definitely doable, and the rewards are well worth it!

Imagine the skills you're developing. Not only are you becoming a whiz at math, a super-speller, or a budding scientist, you're also turning into a skillful musician. You're learning to multitask and manage your time, which are incredibly valuable skills for the future.

2: Making a Schedule

Making a schedule can be a fantastic first step in balancing music and school. Try to allocate specific time slots for music practice. For example, you could choose to practice for thirty minutes after school before starting your homework, or after dinner.

Just remember to be realistic and flexible. It's okay to adjust your schedule if you have an important test coming up or if you're feeling particularly tired one day. What's important is to find a routine that works well for you and stick to it as best you can.

3: The Homework-Music Dance

With homework, things can get a bit tricky, right? But, here's a tip: try to see your music practice as a fun break from your homework rather than a chore. After studying for a while, playing your instrument can feel like a refreshing pause.

This doesn't mean you should rush through your homework to get to music or vice versa. Both require your attention and dedication. Learning to give each its due time is a big part of the balance.

4: School Activities and Music

School is not just about homework. There are sports, clubs, friends, and countless activities to enjoy. And, that's great! Being part of different activities helps you grow in all sorts of ways.

But remember, it's okay if you can't be part of every single activity. If music is important to you, it's perfectly fine to prioritize it. You might choose to join the school band instead of the soccer team, or maybe you'll find a way to do both, even if it means a bit less free time. It's all about finding what makes you happiest.

5: The Power of Patience and Persistence

In all this, patience and persistence are your friends. Some days will be tough. There might be times when you feel overwhelmed with a tricky piece of music or a challenging school project. And that's okay!

Take a deep breath, and remind yourself that it's okay to take things one step at a time. Every great musician, every successful person, has faced challenges. It's facing them, and persisting, that helps us grow.

6: The Joy of Music

Most importantly, always remember the joy of playing music. If you ever feel that your practice is becoming more of a chore, it might be time to mix things up. Try a new song, improvise, or just spend some time messing around on your instrument. Keep the joy alive!

So, young musicians, remember that balancing music and school is a journey. It's about learning to juggle, being patient with yourself, and finding joy in both music and school. You're building fantastic skills and habits that will help you not only in school and music, but also in life!

possibilities for studying music in higher education

Welcome back, superstar musicians! You've been learning, practicing, and growing. Now, let's venture into the future a little and explore the wide world of studying music in higher education. It's never too early to dream big, right?

1: Why Study Music?

First off, why study music? Well, if you love playing your instrument, learning new pieces, and even composing your own songs, studying music might be right up your alley! It's a chance to dive deeper, learn from professionals, and perhaps even make music your career one day. Pretty cool, isn't it?

2: Types of Music Degrees

When it comes to studying music, there's a whole orchestra of options! You might choose a Bachelor of Music, which is typically a four-year degree, focusing on performance, composition, or music education.

Then there's the Bachelor of Arts in Music, where you'll study music, but also other subjects from the arts or sciences. This degree is perfect for those who love music but also have other academic interests.

Want to teach music? A Bachelor of Music Education might

be the right fit! This degree prepares you for teaching music in schools, directing school bands, choirs, or orchestras.

3: Music Conservatories

Have you heard of music conservatories? These are schools dedicated solely to studying and performing music. In conservatories, your days would be filled with music theory classes, ensemble practice, solo practice, and perhaps even composing your own pieces!

4: Combining Music with Other Subjects

Now, if you love music, but also love another subject - say biology or history or graphic design - don't fret! Many universities offer double major programs, allowing you to study two subjects you're passionate about. Music and Math? Why not! Piano and Physics? You bet!

5: Scholarships and Funding

Studying music in higher education can be costly, but there are numerous scholarships, grants, and financial aid options available for talented and dedicated students. So, don't let the potential cost deter you. If music is your passion, there are ways to make it happen!

6: Careers in Music

By studying music in higher education, you're opening doors to numerous exciting careers. You could become a professional performer, playing in orchestras or bands, or even going solo. Or, you might decide to teach, helping others discover the joy of music. And let's not forget about music therapy, conducting, composing, or even working in the music industry!

So there you have it! Studying music in higher education is like entering a huge music festival with endless stages to explore. It's a world full of excitement, opportunities, and, of course, beautiful music!

12 / the professional world of music

explanation of the music industry and how it operates

ARE you ready to rock into a new musical adventure? Today, we're going to discover the fascinating world of the music industry. Now you might think, "That sounds complicated!", but don't worry, we'll break it down into fun, easy-to-understand bits. Are you ready? Then let's hit the play button!

1: What is the Music Industry?

In a nutshell, the music industry is all about creating, recording, selling, and performing music. Imagine it as a massive concert stage with different players like musicians, producers, record labels, concert promoters, music stores, and even fans, all playing their part in making the music world go round.

2: Making and Recording Music

It all starts with musicians creating music. This could be anything from a catchy pop song to a moving classical composition. Once the music is written, it's time to hit the recording studio. Here, with the help of sound engineers and producers, the song comes to life. Think of a producer as a music wizard, adding a touch of magic to make the song sound just right!

3: Record Labels

Next, enter the record labels. They're like the conductors of this orchestra, coordinating different parts of the process. They work with artists to record and produce albums, make music videos, and promote the music to the public. Record labels might be big ones known all around the world, or smaller independent ("indie") labels.

4: Getting Music to the Fans

Once the music is recorded and packaged into an album, it's time to get it to you, the fans! This can happen in several ways. Traditionally, this was done through music stores selling CDs or vinyl records. Nowadays, digital platforms, like music streaming services, are super popular. You can listen to your favorite songs anytime, anywhere!

5: Live Music and Concerts

Of course, we can't forget about live music! Concert promoters organize live performances, ranging from small gigs in local venues to massive music festivals. These events are super important for artists to connect with fans and share their music directly.

6: Other Important Players

There are also music managers, who help guide artists' careers, music publishers who handle the rights of songs, and music journalists who write about new releases and concerts. They all add their own unique notes to this grand symphony!

The music industry might seem big and a bit complex, but remember, at its core, it's all about sharing music and connecting people. It's about that magical moment when you discover a new favorite song, when you sing along to the radio, or when you feel like a song perfectly captures how you're feeling.

potential paths to becoming a professional musician

If you've ever dreamed about standing on a stage, basking in the applause, and sharing your music with the world, then this chapter is your backstage pass to those dreams. Today, we'll explore the different paths you can take to become a professional musician. Ready to tune in? Let's get started!

1: A Symphony of Choices

The first thing you need to know is there's no one 'right way' to become a professional musician. The music world is like a vast orchestra, with each musician playing their own unique part. Just as there are many different instruments to play, there are many different ways to start your music career.

2: The Classical Path

One common path is through classical music education. This often involves starting young, learning an instrument like the violin, piano, or flute, and practicing a lot (and we mean a lot!). Many classical musicians also attend music conservatories, special schools that provide intensive training in music.

3: The School Band or Choir Path

Another path is through school bands or choirs. These provide great opportunities to learn how to play an instrument or sing, read sheet music, and perform as part of a group. Plus, they're loads of fun!

4: The Self-Taught Path

Don't forget the self-taught path! Some musicians learn to play an instrument or sing without formal lessons. Instead, they learn by watching others, practicing on their own, and using resources like online tutorials. This route allows for plenty of creativity and experimentation.

5: The Songwriting Path

What about those who want to create their own songs? Songwriting is a wonderful path to explore! Whether it's jotting down lyrics in a notebook or composing melodies on a keyboard, songwriting allows you to express your thoughts and emotions through music.

6: The Technology Path

In our digital age, there's also the technology path. This involves creating music using computers and software. This can range from electronic music production to creating soundtracks for video games and movies.

7: Mixing and Matching Paths

Remember, you don't have to stick to just one path. Many musicians mix and match these paths, combining classical training with songwriting, or school band experience with technology skills. The key is to find what you love and pursue it passionately.

Each of these paths requires hard work, practice, and a love of music. But guess what? You're already on the path by reading this book and showing an interest in music. Give yourself a round of applause!

13 /
overcoming obstacles

AS YOU JOURNEY through your exciting path of music, it's normal to encounter some rough patches. Just as every song has a unique rhythm, every musician faces unique challenges. Today, we're going to explore these common hurdles and discuss some cool strategies to leap over them. Ready? Let's dive in!

1: The Challenge of Practice

At times, practicing can feel like climbing a mountain. Maybe you get bored easily, feel too tired, or just can't find the time. Don't worry, this is normal. Try setting specific, achievable goals, such as mastering a particular piece of music or practicing for a certain amount of time each day. Also, make practice fun! Create a playlist of your favorite songs to learn or challenge yourself to compose a melody. Remember, every minute spent practicing is a step toward your musical dreams!

2: The Challenge of Frustration

It's easy to get frustrated when progress seems slow or when a piece of music feels too difficult. The key to tackling frustration is patience. Remember, every great musician once started as a beginner. When you hit a tough spot, take a break, breathe deeply, and then try again. If you're still struggling, ask for help. That's what your music teacher is there for!

3: The Challenge of Performance Anxiety

Getting nervous before a performance is as common as a C Major chord in pop songs! One way to overcome stage fright is by practicing in front of friends or family before the actual performance. Visualization techniques can also be helpful. Close your eyes, imagine yourself on stage, playing perfectly and receiving applause. Do this a few times before the performance and you'll feel more confident.

4: The Challenge of Comparison

It's easy to compare ourselves with others, especially in the world of music. But remember, everyone's musical journey is unique. Instead of comparing, try to focus on your own progress. Celebrate your improvements, no matter how small they seem. You're your own musician, and that's pretty cool!

5: The Challenge of Staying Motivated

There might be days when your motivation hits a sour note. When that happens, remind yourself why you fell in love with music in the first place. Listen to your favorite songs, go to a concert, or watch a music-related movie. Reconnecting with your passion for music can strike a chord of motivation.

6: The Challenge of Balancing Music with Other Responsibilities

Balancing music with school, homework, and other activities can be like juggling balls while playing the piano—tricky! But with good time management, you can hit the right balance. Try creating a schedule that includes time for school, music practice, and also fun activities. Remember, it's important to take breaks and have time just to relax and enjoy life.

In our musical journey, just like in a piece of music, there are highs and lows, fast and slow tempos, easy and difficult sections. It's okay to face challenges—it's all part of the journey. The most important thing is to keep playing, keep learning, and keep loving music.

Just think about your favorite song. There might be a note or two that are a bit tricky to hit, or a rhythm that's tough to master. But when all these notes come together, they create a beautiful melody. That's just like your music journey. Each challenge you overcome is a note in your own beautiful melody.

conclusion: your unique music journey

Every melody begins with a single note. Every symphony starts with a single stroke on an instrument. And every musical journey - yours included - commences with a spark of passion, that tiny flame in your heart that whispers, "Hey, I love music." And you know what? That's pretty amazing! This chapter is all about encouraging you to fan that flame into a roaring blaze of creativity and excitement. It's about taking your unique musical journey and letting it lead you to places you've only dreamed of.

Remember this, you are not just another music student. You are a future musician with a voice that is uniquely yours, and music is a fantastic way for you to express yourself. Think about it. In what other language can you 'say' something without uttering a single word, yet still make people feel so much? That's the magic of music.

Now, when I say 'musician', don't think that you have to be on a big stage with thousands of fans (although that would be super cool, wouldn't it?). Being a musician can mean strumming your guitar on your porch, creating a symphony with your school orchestra, writing songs in your bedroom, or even singing in the shower. Being a musician simply means creating music that means something to you.

Conclusion: Your Unique Music Journey

Your musical journey is a path that will take you places you might not expect. You might discover you love playing jazz on a saxophone or that you have a knack for writing catchy pop songs. You might find joy in the quiet concentration of classical piano or the energetic strumming of a ukulele. Remember, there's no right or wrong way to follow your passion for music. The best kind of music is the one that you love to play.

Sometimes, you might feel that your musical journey is a steep climb. You might stumble on a challenging piece or struggle with a tricky rhythm. Remember that every musician - even the ones who perform on big stages - have faced the same struggles. Don't get disheartened. Each struggle is a stepping stone that's helping you grow as a musician. Embrace them, learn from them, and keep going.

I encourage you to be brave. Try different instruments. Experiment with different genres. Write a song, even if you think it's silly. Share your music with others, even if it makes you feel a little nervous. This is YOUR musical journey. Make it as colorful and varied as you can.

It's also important to remember that while music can be a fantastic journey, it should also be fun. Never let the joy of playing music get lost in the quest for perfection. Sure, hitting the right notes is important, but so is enjoying the process. After all, the best performances come from musicians who love what they're doing.

And finally, know that your musical journey is yours and yours alone. Don't compare your progress with anyone else's. Don't worry if someone else can play a piece faster, or if they know more songs. Your musical journey is not a race, it's a path of self-expression and personal growth. So, focus on how far you've come, not how far others have gone.

Your passion for music is a gift. Nurture it, celebrate it, and let it take you on an incredible journey. Remember, every melody starts with a single note, and every musical journey begins with a spark of passion. You've got the spark.

appendices

glossary

As we reach the end of our wonderful journey together, it's time to round off our exploration of the enchanting world of music. And what better way to do that than by mastering some musical jargon? That's right! We're going to dive into a glossary of musical terms. These words and phrases are like secret keys that unlock deeper understanding and appreciation of music. Ready to add some new words to your musical vocabulary? Let's get started!

1. Allegro: This is a tempo marking that means 'fast' and 'lively'. If you see this on your sheet music, it's time to play with some pep in your step!

2. Bar: Also known as a measure, a bar is a segment of time in a piece of music defined by a given number of beats.

3. Chord: This is when three or more different notes are played together. It's like a mini band happening right on your instrument!

4. Duet: This is a piece of music written for two musicians to perform together. So, grab a friend and let the music flow.

5. Ensemble: This is a group of musicians who play together. It can be as small as two people or as large as an orchestra!

Appendices

6. Forte: When you see this term, play loud and proud. It means 'strong' in Italian, and in music, it means to play a note or a section forcefully.

7. Harmony: This is the combination of different musical notes played or sung at the same time to produce a pleasing sound. It's like a musical version of a rainbow!

8. Interval: The distance between two notes is called an interval. It could be as close as one step away on the piano or as far as an entire octave.

9. Melody: This is the main tune in a piece of music, usually the part you find yourself humming long after the song is over.

10. Note: The building block of music! It's a symbol that represents the duration and pitch of a sound.

11. Octave: This is the distance between one musical note and another with half or double its frequency. It's like meeting your note's twin on a different step of the music ladder!

12. Pace: This refers to the speed of the music. It's like the heartbeat of a song.

13. Rhythm: This is the pattern of sound and silence in music. If music is a painting, rhythm is the brushstrokes that bring it to life.

14. Scale: A series of notes arranged in ascending or descending order. It's like a musical staircase!

15. Tempo: This is the speed of the underlying beat in a piece of music.

16. Verse: In songwriting, a verse is usually a repeated section that holds the main story of a song. It's where the tale of the tune unfolds!

17. Vibrato: This is a slight variation in pitch that makes the note wobble just a bit, adding richness and emotion to the sound.

18. Waltz: A dance in 3/4 time with a strong accent on the first beat, and traditionally danced to ballroom music.

19. Xylophone: A musical instrument in the percussion

Appendices

family. It's made up of wooden bars of different lengths that make different pitches when struck.

20. Yodel: A form of singing that involves repeated changes in pitch during a single note. It originated in the Central Alps, and yes, it's as fun as it sounds!

21. Zither: It's a stringed instrument, with strings stretched over a thin, flat body. It's a pretty cool instrument that can make a lot of different sounds, from plucking individual strings to strumming like a guitar.

Alright, you've now got a whole load of musical terms under your belt. Remember, these words and phrases aren't just cool to know—they can help you communicate with other musicians, understand your sheet music, and bring a deeper appreciation to the music you listen to and play. Learning them is like learning a new language, a language that can express things beyond words.

Before we wrap up, just remember one thing: this isn't the end. It's just the beginning! The wonderful world of music is vast and full of endless adventures. Take these words you've learned, your love for music, and keep exploring. Let the music guide you. You're a musician now, and that's a journey that never truly ends.

And hey, why not use some of these terms in your daily life? Next time you and a friend play a piece together, you can tell them, "Hey, let's play this bit in allegro," or "I'll take the melody here, you harmonize." You'll sound super professional and on top of your game. Plus, it's fun to throw around your knowledge!

In the grand symphony of life, you're now ready to play your part with gusto. Be brave, be bold, and above all, keep the music playing. For now, though, that's our coda - the final passage in this part of your musical journey. But remember, in music as in life, every ending is just a new beginning waiting to be played. So, go ahead and play on, because your music has the power to light up the world!

Appendices

resources

Picture this: you've been practicing for hours in your room, mastering scales, honing your ear, and working on your rhythm. You've progressed well, but you want to take it a step further. Where do you go? What can you do? Good news! There are a ton of music schools, online resources, and apps available to help you on your musical journey.

Let's start with music schools. These are institutions where you can learn more about music theory, playing an instrument, singing, and even composing your own tunes.

1. Juilliard School: Based in New York City, this is one of the most prestigious performing arts schools in the world. It's quite competitive but offers excellent opportunities.

2. Berklee College of Music: Located in Boston, this school is known for its contemporary music programs, including jazz, pop, and rock.

3. Royal College of Music: This London-based school is renowned for its classical music programs.

4. Local Community Music Schools: Don't worry if these big names seem out of reach. There are many local community schools that offer fantastic music programs, and they're definitely worth exploring.

Remember, it's important to choose a school that fits your style and goals. Each school has its strengths, so find one that aligns with your musical aspirations!

Now let's look at some online resources. The internet is filled with platforms offering free and paid resources that can supplement your music education.

1. YouTube: Channels like Adam Neely, Aimee Nolte Music, and TwoSet Violin provide a wealth of information, tutorials, and musical humor.

2. MusicTheory.net: A great website to learn the basics of music theory, with plenty of interactive exercises to practice what you've learned.

3. TakeLessons Blog: This site offers tips, tricks, and advice on playing various instruments, singing, and even writing music.

And don't forget about apps! There are many apps available that can help you practice, learn new concepts, or even write your own music.

1. Yousician: This app offers interactive lessons for guitar, piano, bass, ukulele, and singing.

2. Simply Piano: A great app for beginners learning piano. It listens to your piano and gives feedback in real time.

3. GarageBand: An excellent tool for composing your own music. You can play around with a vast array of instruments and even record your own tracks!

As you can see, there are a plethora of resources at your fingertips. Each of these tools brings something unique to your musical journey. They can provide you with new ways to learn and express your creativity.

Remember, though, all these resources are tools to help you on your journey. It's up to you to take the initiative. Practice consistently, explore different kinds of music, and don't be afraid to make mistakes. After all, it's through mistakes that we learn and grow.

further reading and viewing

Now, as you step forth on your exciting musical journey, you might be wondering, "What now?" Well, the answer is simple, and it's in your hands. You have been introduced to an array of knowledge, tools, resources, and have even been given advice by accomplished musicians. But remember, while this book may be nearing its final page, your personal music story is just beginning.

Let's recap on some of the amazing resources you have for your musical journey:

1. Music Schools: These are great places to learn, meet fellow

music enthusiasts, and even perform. Schools such as Juilliard School, Berklee College of Music, and The Royal Conservatory of Music offer a wealth of programs and classes to learn from.

2. Online Resources: Websites like MusicTheory.net, Coursera, and even YouTube have countless lessons on different instruments, music theory, and more. They can be a convenient way to learn at your own pace and in the comfort of your own home.

3. Apps: Technology has made learning music more accessible than ever. Apps like Yousician, Simply Piano, and Ultimate Guitar can make practice fun and interactive.

4. Books: You've already started with this one, but there are many more out there! Books can provide you with a deeper understanding of music theory, history, and even the lives of famous musicians.

5. Films and Documentaries: Watching films and documentaries about music can be both entertaining and educational. You can learn about the lives of musicians, the process of making music, and the history of different music genres.

Remember, while all these resources are valuable, they are just tools to assist you. The true magic happens when you apply what you've learned. So, go ahead, pick up your instrument, start practicing, and don't forget to have fun!

Whether you aspire to perform in a grand concert hall or just enjoy playing for yourself, each note you play adds to the beautiful symphony of the world. Your music can express your feelings, tell a story, or even bring people together. The possibilities are as limitless as your creativity.

Remember that making music is not a race, but a journey. There might be challenging practice sessions, difficult pieces, and the occasional stage fright, but every great musician has faced these. Keep the words of Ludwig Van Beethoven in mind: "To play a wrong note is insignificant; to play without passion is inexcusable."

Appendices

As we turn over to the final pages of this book, know that this is not the end, but the beginning of your unique musical journey. Keep exploring, stay curious, and most importantly, enjoy every step of your musical adventure. The world awaits your melody!